THE CHICAGO RACE RIOTS

THE
CHICAGO RACE RIOTS
JULY, 1919

BY
CARL SANDBURG

WITH AN INTRODUCTORY NOTE
BY WALTER LIPPMANN

NEW YORK
HARCOURT, BRACE AND HOWE
1919

TITLE PAGE OF FIRST EDITION,
PUBLISHED ON NOVEMBER 24, 1919

CARL SANDBURG

The Chicago Race Riots

JULY, 1919

With a Preface by
RALPH McGILL
and an Introductory Note by
WALTER LIPPMANN

HARCOURT, BRACE & WORLD, INC.

New York

B.4.70

LIBRARY OF CONGRESS CATALOG CARD NUMBER: 70-85014

PRINTED IN THE UNITED STATES OF AMERICA

ISBN 0-15-117150-5

CONTENTS

PREFACE

HOW much do cities, a people, a nation learn in fifty years?

Not much.

Half a century ago, on a hot and steaming July day, a Negro boy swam past an invisible line of segregation at one of Chicago's public beaches. He was stoned, knocked unconscious and drowned. Police shrugged off requests from Negroes that the rock-throwing white men be arrested. After the body was pulled from the water fighting was renewed. This and other forms of violence did not stop for three days. Thirty-four men had then been killed, twenty Negroes, fourteen whites. An uncounted number, more than a hundred, had been wounded. Several houses in the "black belt" had been burned and damaged.

A young reporter and writer, Carl Sandburg, was assigned to write a series of newspaper articles on the riots. They were published in book form in 1919 by a newly established publishing firm, Harcourt, Brace and Howe.

It is from these reports that we learn that a city, a nation, a people don't learn very much, if anything, about themselves in half a century.

There were commissions in 1919. They discovered there was much poverty. They found that the hearses haul more babies out of poverty areas than from those where the wages and hours are better.

There were other facts revealed by investigation.

Chicago's black-belt population of 50,000 had more than doubled, to at least 125,000, by 1919. (The black population was 812,637 in the 1960 census. An early estimate for 1969 was near one million.)

In 1919 no new tenements or housing had been built in Chicago to absorb the pressure of doubled population.

The black doughboys had come home from France and war cantonments. They had a new voice—or wanted to have one.

Thousands of Negroes had migrated from the South where "neither a world war for democracy, nor the Croix de Guerre, nor three gold chevrons, nor any number of wound stripes, assures them of the right to vote or to have their votes counted or to participate responsibly in the elective determinations of the American republic."

Housing, war psychology, politics and organization of labor and jobs fueled the Chicago riot in 1919.

That and several other riots of half a century ago were a good school of experience. But we were all dropouts. Few Americans learned anything.

The decade of the 1920s was about to begin—the era of wonderful nonsense.

During that span of stock-market frenzy, few north

of the Mason-Dixon Line were to pay any attention to the cotton South—where the boll weevil had arrived. He had made a long journey of many years from South America into Mexico, across the Rio Grande and the waters of the Mississippi, into the region where for so long a time cotton had been king. The boll weevil makes tiny noises. It lays an egg in a cotton boll. The hatched-out weevil chews away—just enough to kill the boll. The clicking of the stock-market ticker tapes drowned out the weevil chorus.

By 1922 and 1923 cotton plantations and farms that had been producing thousands of bales of cotton were turning out 150 or 220 bales. By the late 1920s many of the two-storied houses were empty and deserted. So were thousands of cabins and shacks where the tenants and sharecroppers had lived. The hearthstones about which families had warmed themselves in grief and hope were cold. Doors swung drunkenly in the wind. Many a man owing "the man" and the county-seat store with its marked-up prices had vanished silently in the night. Numerous cabins were burned. Careless hunters, huddling inside in a sudden slash of November rain, would start fires that sometimes got out of hand. There were hundreds of lonely chimneys in the 1920s. (They were even lonelier in the 1930s.) Nearly 200,000 men, black and white, left the South in the 1920s—the boll-weevil decade. Most of them went to Dee-troit, to Akron, to Pittsburgh, to South Chicago . . . anywhere there were jobs that unskilled hands could do.

The very corrosiveness of the Depression years of

fear, unemployment and grief brought a temporary halt
to most of the migration from the South. Those years
also delayed the development of resistance to racism that
was plainly visible in the riots of 1919.

A. Mitchell Palmer, U.S. attorney general of that period, was far ahead of a later Joe McCarthy in creating
a "red" hysteria. Woodrow Wilson sought to calm
Palmer. He could not. The Palmer raids and charges
yielded no results save that he was for a while a hero.
The costly effect of A. Mitchell Palmer's becoming a
hero was that he gave free rein to all the ugliness and
violence in America.

Anti-Semites had their inning. They printed and dis-
tributed "The Protocols of the Elders of Zion," long before proved to be one of the more hoary fakes. The
anti-Semites aroused the more simple minded with tales
of a Jewish conspiracy. The anti-Catholics were also
in full bloom. They blamed the war on the Catholics and
the Negro. They printed smears and lies about Catholics
and the plot for the Pope to come to America and take
over. The Ku Klux Klan staged a revival out of Atlanta.
America was so spiritually bankrupt that the nightshirt
and mask business flourished nationally. The Klan
stronghold was in Dixie. But it also established strong
centers in Indiana, Oklahoma and Oregon. Never have
all the peddlers of hate and lies had so great a harvest.
The Negro suffered most.

Lynchings reached a crescendo in the South. Mob
violence had been a part of Reconstruction. In exchange

for Southern support to make Rutherford B. Hayes president in 1876, the North's political and economic power structures had abandoned the Negro. He was literally "turned back to states' rights." Black codes, disfranchisement and segregation by law were quick developments. That horror—the mob at a frenzy of bloody killing—was accompanied by laws and states' rights decisions that declared the Negro inferior and defined his "place." These mob activities also sent Negroes northward in search for jobs that were less and less to be found in the South, where fear and the boll weevil were at work.

But it was not merely the Negro who left. He was the more numerous in out-migration. But the poor white went, too—and all the Negro's liabilities also were his. He had but one advantage—he had a white skin and he had been reared to believe this gave him supremacy and status.

So, when Negro migrants came asking for jobs at factories and mills, the white job holders, especially the immigrants from Dixie, reacted with fury. In east St. Louis in 1917, forty-seven persons, mostly Negroes, were killed and hundreds more wounded in vicious race riots growing out of resentment against Negro employment.

In July of 1919, in Washington, the nation's capital, several thousand troops were called out to halt the white-black rioting. That same summer there were riots in New York and Omaha—all in addition to those in Chicago. In the South that summer there were seven riots. Most of them grew out of the "impudence" of returned Negro veterans demanding their rights as citizens.

Reporter Carl Sandburg's accounts were not easy to get. They are not always, as he himself said, in exact sequence. But it was a fine, down-to-earth job.

Among the many revealing sentences from his reports, one will illustrate:

"During 1918 there had been 30,000 applications for jobs and 10,000 placed. . . . There is a steady influx of colored population from the Southern states. . . ."

Let us go back also to some lynching headlines out of the year 1919:

April 5, 1919—Blakely, Georgia: "When Private William Little, a Negro soldier returning from the war, arrived at the railroad station here a few weeks ago, he was met by a band of whites who ordered him to remove his uniform and walk home in his underwear. Bystanders persuaded the men to release him. Little continued to wear the uniform as he had no other clothes. . . . Anonymous notes reached him warning him to quit wearing it. Yesterday Private Little was found dead, his body badly beaten, on the outskirts of town. He was wearing his uniform."

May 1, 1919—Shreveport, Louisiana: "A Vicksburg, Shreveport and Pacific train was held up by an armed mob here today, about five miles from Monroe, and George Holden, accused of writing a note to a white woman, was taken from the train and shot. . . . The note was in plain handwriting. According to friends, Holden was not able to read or write."

May 15, 1919—Vicksburg, Mississippi: "Lloyd Clay, Negro laborer, was roasted to death here last night. He had been accused of entering a white woman's room. . . . A mob of between 800 and 1,000 men and women removed the prisoner from the jail. He was taken to the corner of Clay and Farmer Streets, covered with oil, set afire and hoisted to an elm tree. Bullets were fired into the body. . . ."

These are samples.

During the first six months of 1919, lynchings declined as against the first half of 1918. The total was a mere twenty-eight in comparison with thirty-five in 1918. Of those lynched in the first half of 1919, one was a Negro woman.

The exodus from South to North continued. The Depression decade slowed it. But by 1940 it was at a greater peak than ever. It was speeded again by World War II, when lend-lease factories working overtime were a tremendous magnet for labor. The disaster at Pearl Harbor turned much of this tide of labor westward to build planes, ships and weapons for retaking the Pacific.

This out-movement of people has never stopped. Indeed, the largest migrant movement was in 1950–1960. Since 1940 almost four million Negroes have left the South. When the war plants closed they stayed on, for they had nowhere else to go. They filled up the central cities. They are the ghetto, the slum people—they and enclaves of poor "hillbilly" whites. The latter, also cheated and degraded by the system, no longer have a meaningful skin value.

Their bitterness and alienation increases.

In 1940 about 70 per cent of all the Negroes in America were in the South. And now? Maybe 50 per cent. We shall need to wait for the 1970 census. . . .

Carl Sandburg's reports of half a century ago are a serious indictment of us as a people. We are again confronted with our incredible neglect of social facts and our lack of awareness of their meaning.

One of his chapters reproduces the demands of the National Association for the Advancement of Colored People following the Chicago riots. They are mild compared with those of 1968. One wonders what might have happened to the social, political and economic health of America had those modest demands been met half a century ago.

There cannot be a repetition of the past. There will be renewed attempts to thwart, delay or ignore the laws and the gains. They can hardly succeed.

In 1919 there were few Negroes registered to vote—and almost none in the South. In 1944 there were about a quarter of a million Negroes registered in the South. The voter registration laws were not enacted by the Congress until 1964 and were not implemented until 1965. In 1964 there were over two million black voters registered in the states of the old Confederacy. In 1969 the total is certainly three and a quarter million. There now are 385 Negroes elected to public office in the South—the heaviest concentration of such officials in the nation.

The melancholy aspect of this progress is that the South and most of its congressmen, senators, public leaders, editors and clergymen opposed the advances. But they came on. (Open-housing legislation, for example, was stalled until the assassination of Dr. Martin Luther King, Jr.)

The lesson of 1919 and of later years has not been fully learned. There still is resistance to creating an unsegregated society in which the Negro is free to be his own self—not an imitation white man, but a Negro or black citizen of his country.

This re-issue of Chicago's riot reports of fifty years ago is a bitter-tasting medicine. It indicts us as a people addicted to folly and violent resistance to healthful social and political change.

If the gentle reader is in need of a chill tonic, then let him open up the bottle of Carl Sandburg's report of fifty years ago and take a dose.

Ralph McGill

ATLANTA, GEORGIA
JANUARY, 1969

INTRODUCTORY NOTE

TO record the background of an event, infinitely more disgraceful than that Mexican banditry or Red Terror about which we are all so virtuously indignant, is sufficient reason for republishing these articles by Carl Sandburg. They are first hand, and they are sympathetic, and they will move those who will allow themselves to be moved.

Moved not alone to indignation, though that is needed, but to thought. It is not possible, I think, to examine this record without concluding that the race problem as we know it is really a by-product of our planless, disordered, bedraggled, drifting democracy. Until we have learned to house everybody, employ everybody at decent wages in a self-respecting status, guarantee his civil liberties, and bring education and play to him, the bulk of our talk about "the race problem" will remain a sinister mythology. In a dirty civilization the relation between black men and white will be a dirty one. In a clean civilization the two races can conduct their business together cleanly, and not until then.

Certainly the idea must go that in order to segregate the races biologically it is necessary to degrade and ter-

rorize one of them. For those who degrade and terror-
ize are inevitably themselves degraded and terror-
stricken. It is only the parvenue, the snob, the coward
who is forever proclaiming his superiority. And by
proclaiming it he evokes imitation in his victim. Hence
the peculiar oppressiveness of recently oppressed peoples in Europe. Hence the Negro who desires to be an
imitation white man. Hence again the determination to
suppress the Negro who attempts to imitate the white
man. For so long as the status of the white man is in
every way superior to that of the colored, the advancement of the colored man can mean nothing but an at-
tempt to share the white man's social privileges. From
this arises that terrible confusion between the idea of
social equality and the idea of social mixture.

Since permanent degradation is unthinkable, and
amalgamation undesirable for both blacks and whites,
the ideal would seem to lie in what might be called race
parallelism. Parallel lines may be equally long and
equally straight; they do not join except in infinity,
which is further away than anyone need worry about
just now. We shall have to work out with the Negro a
relationship which gives him complete access to all the
machinery of our common civilization, and yet allows
him to live so that no Negro need dream of a white
heaven and of bleached angels. Pride of race will come
to the Negro when a dark skin is no longer associated
with poverty, ignorance, misery, terror and insult. When
this pride arises every white man in America will be the

happier for it. He will be able then, as he is not now, to enjoy the finest quality of civilized living—the fellowship of different men.

Walter Lippmann

WHITESTONE, LONG ISLAND
AUGUST 26, 1919

THE CHICAGO RACE RIOTS

[I]

THE CHICAGO RACE RIOTS

THE so-called race riots in Chicago during the last week of July, 1919, started on a Sunday at a bathing beach. A colored boy swam across an imaginary segregation line. White boys threw rocks at him and knocked him off a raft. He was drowned. Colored people rushed to a policeman and asked for the arrest of the boys throwing stones. The policeman refused. As the dead body of the drowned boy was being handled, more rocks were thrown, on both sides. The policeman held on to his refusal to make arrests. Fighting then began that spread to all the borders of the Black Belt. The score at the end of three days was recorded as twenty negroes dead, fourteen white men dead, and a number of negro houses burned.

The riots furnished an excuse for every element of Gangland to go to it and test their prowess by the most ancient ordeals of the jungle. There was one section of the city that supplied more white hoodlums than any other section. It was the district around the stockyards and packing houses.

I asked Maclay Hoyne, states attorney of Cook County, "Does it seem to you that you get more tough birds from out around the stockyards than anywhere else in Chicago?" And he answered that more bank robbers, payroll bandits, automobile bandits, high-waymen and strong-arm crooks come from this particular district than any other that has come to his notice during seven years of service as chief prosecuting official.

And I recalled that a few years ago a group of people from the University of Chicago came over into the stockyards district and made a survey. They went into one neighborhood and asked at every house about how the people lived—and died. They found that seven times as many white hearses haul babies along the streets here as over in the lake shore district a mile east. Their statement of scientific fact was that the infant mortality was seven times higher here proportionately, than a mile to the east in a district where housing and wages are different.

So on the one hand we have blind lawless government failing to function through policemen ignorant of Lincoln, the Civil War, the Emancipation Proclamation, and a theory sanctioned and baptized in a storm of red blood. And on the other hand we have a gaunt involuntary poverty from which issues the hoodlum.

At least three conditions marked the events of violence in Chicago in July, 1919, and gave the situation a character essentially different from the backgrounds of other riots. Here are factors that give the Chicago flare-up historic import:

1. The Black Belt population of 50,000 in Chicago was more than doubled during the war. No new houses or tenements were built. Under pressure of war industry the district, already notoriously overcrowded and swarming with slums, was compelled to have and hold in its human dwelling apparatus more than twice as many people as it held before the war.

2. The Black Belt of Chicago is probably the strongest effective unit of political power, good or bad, in America. It connects directly with a city administration decisive in its refusal to draw the color line, and a mayor whose opponents failed to defeat him with the covert circulation of the epithet of "nigger lover." To such a community the black doughboys came back from France and the cantonment camps. Also it is known that hundreds—it may be thousands—have located in Chicago in the hope of permanent jobs and homes in preference to returning south of Mason and Dixon's line, where neither a world war for democracy, nor the Croix de Guerre, nor three gold chevrons, nor any number of wound stripes, assures them of the right to vote or to have their votes counted or to participate responsibly in the elective determinations of the American republic.

3. Thousands of white men and thousands of colored men stood together during the riots, and through the public statements of white and colored officials of the Stockyards Labor Council asked the public to witness that they were shaking hands as "brothers" and could not be counted on for any share in the mob shouts and

ravages. This was the first time in any similar crisis in an American community that a large body of mixed nationalities and races—Poles, Negroes, Lithuanians, Italians, Irishmen, Germans, Slovaks, Russians, Mexicans, Yankees, Englishmen, Scotchmen—proclaimed that they were organized and opposed to violence between white union men and colored union men.

In any American city where the racial situation is critical at this moment, the radical and active factors probably are (1) housing, (2) politics and war psychology and (3) organization of labor.

The articles that follow are reprints from the pages of the *Chicago Daily News,* which assigned the writer to investigate the situation three weeks before the riots began. Publication of the articles had proceeded two weeks and were approaching the point where a program of constructive recommendations would have been proper when the riots broke and as usual nearly everybody was more interested in the war than how it got loose.

The arrangement of the material herewith is all rather hit or miss, with the stress often in the wrong place, as in much newspaper writing. However, because of the swift movement of events at this hour and because items of information and views of trends here have been asked for in telegrams, letters and phone calls from a number of thoughtful people, they are made conveniently available for such service as they are worth.

[II]

THE BACKGROUND

CHICAGO's "black belt," so called, to-day holds at least 125,000 persons. This is double the number that same district held five years ago, when the world war began.

Chicago is probably the third city in the United States in number of colored persons and, at the lowest, ranks as fifth in this regard, according to estimates of Frederick Rex, municipal reference librarian. The four cities that may possibly exceed Chicago in this population group are New York, which had 91,709 at the last census; Baltimore, with 84,749; Philadelphia, with 84,-459, and Washington, with 94,466. The colored population in all these cities has increased since the last census.

New Orleans, which had 89,262, has decreased instead of gaining, and the same will apply to three other large southern cities where the colored population at the beginning of the war was slightly above 50,000 and just about equal to that of Chicago. These are Birmingham, Ala., Atlanta, Ga., and Memphis, Tenn., all reported to have decreased, while Chicago has gained.

During interviews with some forty persons more or

less expert on the question the lowest estimate of the present colored population of Chicago was 100,000 and the highest 200,000. The figure most commonly agreed on was 125,000. There is no doubt that upward of 150,-000 have arrived here. The number that have departed for other points is unknown.

Under the pressure of the biggest over-crowding problem any race or nation has faced in a Chicago neighborhood, the population of the district is spilling over, or rather is being irresistibly squeezed out into other residence districts.

Such is the immediately large and notable fact touching what is generally called "the race problem."

Other facts pertaining to the situation, each one indicating a trend of importance, are the following:

Local draft board No. 4 in a district surrounding State and 35th streets, containing 30,000 persons, of whom 90 per cent are colored, registered upward of 9,000 and sent 1,850 colored men to cantonments. Of these 1,850 there were only 125 rejections. On Nov. 11, when the armistice was declared, this district had 7,832 men passed by examiners and ready for the call to the colors. So it is clear that in one neighborhood are thousands of strong young men who have been talking to each other on topics more or less intimately related to the questions, "What are we ready to die for? Why do we live? What is democracy? What is the meaning of freedom; of self-determination?"

In barber shop windows and in cigar stores and

haberdasheries are helmets, rifles, cartridges, canteens and haversacks and photographs of negro regiments that were sent to France.

Walk around this district and talk with the black folk and leaders of the black folk. Ask them, "What about the future of the colored people?" The reply that comes most often and the thought that seems uppermost is: "We made the supreme sacrifice; they didn't need any work or fight law for us; our record, like Old Glory, the flag we love because it stands for our freedom, hasn't got a spot on it; we 'come clean'; now we want to see our country live up to the constitution and the declaration of independence."

Soldiers, ministers, lawyers, doctors, politicians, machinists, teamsters, day laborers—this is the inevitable outstanding thought they offer when consulted about tomorrow, next week, next year or the next century for the colored race in America. There is no approaching the matters of housing, jobs or political relations of the colored people to-day without taking consideration of their own vivid conception of what they consider their unquestioned Americanism.

They had one bank three years ago. Now they have five. Three co-operative societies to run stores are forming. Five new weekly papers, two new monthly magazines, seven drug stores, one hospital—all of these have come since Junius B. Wood's encyclopedic recital of negro activities in Chicago appeared in *The Daily News* in December, 1916. Also since then a life insurance company and a building and loan association have been organized. In one district where there were counted sixty-nine neighborhood agencies of demoralization there have been established within two years under negro auspices, a cafe, a drug store, a laundry, a bakery, a shoe repair shop, a tailor shop, a fish market, a dry goods store—all told, twenty-four constructive agencies entered the contest against sixty-nine of the destructive kind.

The colored people of Chicago seem to have more big organizations with fewer press agents and less publicity than any other group in the city. They have, for instance, the largest single protestant church membership in North America in the Olivet Baptist church at South Park avenue and East 31st street. It has more than 8,500 members. The "miscellaneous" local of the Meat Cutters and Butcher Workmen's union, at 43d and State streets, reports that upward of 10,000 colored workmen are affiliated. The People's Movement club has moved into a $50,000 clubhouse, has 2,000 active and 6,000 associate members.

There is apparent an active home buying, home owning movement, with many circumstances indicating that the colored people coming in with the new influx are making preparations to stay, their viewpoint being that of the boll weevil in that famous negro song, "This'll Be My Home." In nearly all circles the opinion is voiced that Chicago is the most liberal all around town in the country, and the constitution of Illinois the most liberal of all state constitutions. And so if they can't make Chicago a good place for their people to live in the colored people wonder where they can go.

Their houses, jobs, politics, their hope and outlook in the "black belt," are topics to be considered in this series of articles.

[III]

THE NEGRO MIGRATION

AT Michigan avenue and East 31st street comes along the street a colored woman and three of her children. Two months ago they lived in Alabama, in a two room hut with a dirt floor and no running water and none of the things known as "conveniences." Barefooted and bareheaded, the children walk along with the mother, casually glancing at Michigan avenue's moving line of motor cars. Suddenly, as in a movie play, a big limousine swings to the curb. A colored man steps out, touches his hat to the mother and children and gives them the surprise of their lives. This is what he says:

"We don't do this up here. It isn't good for us colored folks to send our children out on the streets like this. We're all working together to do the best we can. One thing we're particular about is the way we take the little ones out on the streets.

"They ought to look as if they're washed clean all over. And they ought to have shoes and stockings and hats and clean shirts on. Now you go home and see to that. If you haven't got the money to do it, come and see me. Here's my card."

He gives her the card of a banker and real estate

man at an office where they collect rent monthly from over 1,000 tenants, and where they hold titles in fee simple to the rented properties.

This little incident gives some idea of the task of assimilation Chicago took in the last five years in handling the more than 70,000 colored people who came here in that time, mostly from southern states.

A big brown stone residence in Wabash avenue, of the type that used to be known as "mansions," housed five families from Alabama. They threw their dinner leavings from the back porch. And one night they sat on the front steps and ate watermelon and threw the rinds out past the curbstone. In effect, they thought they were going to live in the packed human metropolis of Chicago just as they had lived "down in Alabam'."

Now they have learned what garbage cans are for. From all sides the organized and intelligent forces of the colored people have hammered home the suggestion that every mistake of one colored man or woman may result in casting a reflection on the whole group. The theory is, "Be clean for your own sake, but remember that every good thing you do goes to the credit of all of us."

It must not be assumed, of course, that the types thus far mentioned are representative of all who come from Alabama or other states of the south. Among the recent arrivals, for example, are a banker, the managing editor of a weekly newspaper, a manual training instructor in the public schools and several men who have made successes in business. It is possible now for Chicago white people to come into contact with colored men who have had years of experience in direct co-operation with Tuskegee and Hampton institutes and with the workings in southern states of the theories of Booker T. Washington, W. E. B. Du Bois and others. The application of these theories is being continued in Chicago.

Willis N. Huggins, an intensely earnest and active worker for the interests of the colored people, is an instructor in manual training at the Wendell Phillips high school. He came from Alabama in 1917.

"I was making a social survey of the northern counties of Alabama through the financial aid of Mrs. Emmons Blaine of Chicago," he said to me. "My work was discontinued because our information collected in that territory would be useless. About one-fourth of the colored people migrated to the north.

"There were 12,000 colored people in Decatur, Ala., before the war. The migration took away 4,000, judging by a house to house canvass I made in various sections of that one city. When they took the notion they just went. You could see hundreds of houses where mattresses, beds, wash bowls and pans were thrown around the back yard after the people got through picking out what they wanted to take along.

"All the railroad trains from big territory farther south came on through Decatur. Some days five and six of these trains came along. The colored people in

Decatur would go to the railroad station and talk with these other people about where they were going. And when the moving fever hit them there was no changing their minds.

"Take Huntsville, only a few miles from Decatur, on a branch line. There they didn't see these twelve coach trains coming through loaded with emigrants. So from Huntsville there was not much emigration.

"In many localities the educated negroes came right along with their people. I rode in September, 1917, with a minister from Monroe, La. This was his second trip. He had been to Boston and organized a church with 100 members of his Louisiana congregation. Now he was taking fifty, all in one coach. I hear that later he made a third trip and has now moved the whole of his original congregation of 300 members up to Boston. He told me that the first group he took to Boston were all naturally inclined to go. The second group made up their minds more slowly. He said that probably they would not have gone at all if it had not been for fears of lynching. A series of lynchings in Texas at that time gave him examples from which to argue that the north was safer for colored people.

"With many who have come north, the attraction of wages and employment is secondary to the feeling that they are going where there are no lynchings. Others say that while they know they would never be lynched in the south and they are not afraid on that score, they do want to go where they are sure there is more equality and opportunity than in the south. The schools in the north are an attraction to others.

"I make these observations from having personally talked with my people in Madison county, Alabama, where there were 10,000 negroes, of whom 5,000 came north in two years."

[IV]

REAL ESTATE

EIGHT bombs or dynamite containers have been ex-
ploded within the last five months on the doorsteps of
buildings in the south division of the city, all of these
buildings being situated in streets adjacent to the residence district popularly called the "black belt," where
the population is about 80 per cent colored. The eight
explosions took place between Feb. 5 and June 13.

The amount of property destroyed by each explosion
varied from $50 to $600. Seven of the cases were investigated by the police of the station situated at Wabash avenue and 48th street, and one was investigated
by the police of the Cottage Grove Avenue station.

The police began their work with two theories in
mind: one that the explosions were the result of race
feeling, the other that there was a clash between two real
estate interests. As a result of their work, the police now
believe that the second theory is the more likely to be
correct.

Facts in this situation to be reckoned with are that
practically every organization of colored people, business, political, social and religious, is making propaganda in favor of the right of the colored people to

buy real estate "wherever the white man's money is good." On the other hand, the only organized and noticeable propaganda among white organizations in this respect is the movement in real estate organizations and neighborhood improvement clubs.

With reference to the effect of colored residents on real estate values, there are two points of view. It is asserted, on one hand, that in all cases where the property owner has kept up the improvements and refused to sell to speculators, his real estate has risen in value. On the other hand, it is contended that colored residents bring down property values in a neighborhood. Both sides point to specific instances in support of their contentions.

L. M. Smith, of the Kenwood Improvement association, a prominent spokesman for real estate interests, and one of those most active in opposition to the movement of colored people eastward in his part of the city, gave the writer the following expression of his views:

"We want to be fair. We want to do what is right. But these people will have to be more or less pacified. At a conference where their representatives were present, I told them we might as well be frank about it, 'you people are not admitted to our society,' I said. Personally, I have no prejudice against them. I have had experience of many years dealing with them, and I'll say this for them: I have never had to foreclose a mortgage on one of them. They have been clean in every way, and always prompt in their payments. But, you know, improvements are coming along the lake shore, the Illinois Central, and all that; we can't have these people coming over here.

"Not one cent has been appropriated by our organization for bombing or anything like that.

"They injure our investments. They hurt our values. I couldn't say how many have moved in, but there's at least a hundred blocks that are tainted. We are not making any threats, but we do say that something must be done. Of course, if they come in as tenants, we can handle the situation fairly easily. But when they get a deed, that's another matter. Be sure to get us straight on that. We want to be fair and do what's right."

Charles S. Duke, a Harvard graduate, former lieutenant of company G, 8th Illinois infantry and a civil engineer in the bridge division of the city department of public works, expresses the view of his people as follows:

"All attempts at segregation bring only discord and resentful opposition. The bombing of the homes of colored citizens is futile. This will neither intimidate any considerable number of them nor stop their moving into a given district. The most certain result is bitter racial antagonism.

"White citizens must be educated out of all hysteria over actual or prospective arrival of colored neighbors. All colored citizens do not make bad neighbors, although in some cases they will not make good ones. It is of the greatest importance, however, both to white and colored people, that real estate dealers should cease to make a business of commercializing racial antagonisms."

During the series of bomb explosions from February 5 to June 13 the police made no arrests. On June 13 they took into custody James Macherol of 4945 South State street and James Turner of 8948 Parnell avenue. The charges were bomb throwing, malicious mischief and carrying explosives without authorization. Their cases have been granted two continuances in Judge Gemmill's court. Turner is a clerk in the real estate office of Dean & Meagher, 320 East 51st street.

Habeas corpus proceedings in behalf of Turner were unsuccessful in a hearing before Judge Pam. One continuance in the Hyde Park court was granted on the plea of the defendant's attorney that an alibi witness had gone for a two weeks' vacation in Minnesota.

In the series of bombings there is little or nothing to indicate a motive to destroy life. In one case a child was killed. The police have evidence that in the flat next door an Italian girl was to be married and jealous suitors had sent threats of violence. The theory is that the dynamiters put the bomb on the wrong doorstep.

[V]

DEMAND FOR NEGRO LABOR

THE demand for colored workers took a slump when the armistice was signed. And the slump went on till April. Then things began to look up. Now there has come a strong movement toward the conditions that held good while the war was on.

At the office of the Chicago Urban league, 3032 South Wabash avenue, where a branch of the United States Employment service is maintained, the office force was finding work for 1,700 to 1,800 men and women each month before the armistice was signed. This figure dropped to 500 in April. In the week ended June 14, Secretary T. Arnold Hill, colored man and graduate of New York university, reports 249 men and thirty-four women, a total of 283, placed. He comments:

"At this rate we should place 1,132 persons a month, as compared with 500 or 600 during the three months period previous."

The following is a specimen of the demand for colored workers on one day in June: Quartermaster's corps, U.S.A., twenty-five men at 45 cents an hour; National Malleable Casting Company, twenty men at 40 cents an hour; South-eastern Coal Company, forty men at piece rates; C., B. & Q. railroad company, ten men at 45 cents an hour; Camp Custer, two hundred men at 45 cents an hour; railroad workers for the state of Washington, fifty men at 45 cents an hour; Turbell Ice Cream company, four men at $19 a week.

A bulletin of the office for June 25 states:

"Unskilled work is plentiful. Jobs in foundries and steel mills, in building and construction work, in light factories and packing houses, keep up a steady demand for semi-skilled laborers."

During 1918 there was a total of 30,000 applications for jobs, and 10,000 persons were placed.

It is believed a record somewhat like this will be maintained again this year; that is, a steady influx of colored population, almost entirely from southern states, will keep on coming and will be absorbed by northern industry. The amount of this influx will not be as large as in the last year or two, but it is expected to be steady. It will have the same steady flow, according to men closely in touch with it, as the stream of immigration from Europe that kept coming to America's shores with such periodic certainty before the war.

Among large employing interests as well as in both white and colored labor circles the expectation is that the northern labor supply will be constantly replenished from the south. The reasons for this are found in conditions described by the immigration and inspection service of the department of labor in a report not as yet made public. From Dr. George Edwin Haynes, a colored man who took a master's degree at Yale and Ph.D. at Columbia, and who is a director of negro economics in the department of labor, comes an advance report on these conditions, as follows:

"Among alien residents in our country large numbers intend to return to their native land. The principal cause is a desire to learn what has befallen their families. Many aliens told investigators they had not heard from their families in four years; that they had sent money home, but had no means of knowing whether it was received or not. Another cause is a desire to ascertain and settle estates of relatives killed during the war.

"Unemployment is still severe in some sections and there is also a desire on the part of many foreigners to return to the land just freed from German or Austrian domination in the belief that opportunities will be better in the new democracies than in the United States.

"In many cities investigation shows that fully 50 per cent of the aliens intend to go back to Europe. A large number of these expect eventually to return to the United States, but many say they will not come back. The clergyman of one foreign church with 1,600 parishioners expects not more than 100 will remain in this country. In an Indiana city with a large Roumanian population, from 40 to 50 per cent want to return to their homeland, Transylvania. Few Poles in the same city expect to return, but 150 of the 600 Serbians wish to go, and it was said that if unemployment became more serious, this number would be increased.

"An investigation by a steel plant showed that 66 per cent of its alien help were married and 64 per cent of them had dependents in the old country. In this plant 61 per cent of all the aliens declared their intention to return to Europe, and of this number 91 per cent said they were going to stay, while only 9 per cent were planning to return to America after their European visit.

"A prominent Hungarian of Chicago estimated that 30,000 unnaturalized Austro-Hungarians live in this city and that 50 per cent would go back to Europe. Out of a Polish population of 15,000, there were 6,000 expected to return. Among Lithuanians there is a strong feeling that if Lithuania becomes independent there will be a large movement back to that country. These figures gathered by the investigation and inspection service of the department of labor show conclusively that large numbers of aliens will leave never to return."

With America helping to rebuild Europe and feed its people, business expansion is a certainty, Dr. Haynes predicts, at the same time asking, "Where is the labor coming from to take the place of the labor that is gone never to return?" Replying, he says: "It isn't coming from China. Somebody has suggested that we bring over 1,000,000 Chinese coolies. Unless we change the laws we passed in the last twenty years, we can't do that. It is not coming from Japan because the Pacific coast states are going to raise such a howl that we cannot change the laws. Furthermore it looks as though we are going to have restriction on immigration from the European countries. So we may get a few Hawaiians, Filipinos, West Indians, but they are colored people. The only great source from which we can develop a new power of labor that is as yet undeveloped, is from the great mass of 12,000,000 negro workers.

"All we are waiting for is the open gate so we may enter into the industrial and agricultural opportunities on the same terms as other workers. That day has arrived. When orders come from France and Belgium and central Europe and South America and Africa to the American factories, it doesn't matter an iota what color the skin of the man whose hand or brain produces that product. The manufacturer is getting more and more to realize that when the pressure comes, as it came during the war, if he can get the labor he doesn't see any color mark on the bank check or the draft that he gets in payment for his goods. Most of this thing we call a race question is down at rock bottom a labor question.

"When the colored man can come into the labor market and bargain for the sale of his services on the same terms as other workers, a great deal of what is termed to-day the 'race question' is going to be settled."

[VI]

NEW INDUSTRIAL OPPORTUNITIES

CONSIDERATION of the question of work for colored people shows that it presents three important features: (1) the opening of doors to new occupations so that skilled men will not have to stay in the common labor group all their lives; (2) getting men and women trained to perform skilled or unskilled labor and coaching them when on a job so that they will hold on; (3) creating a sentiment among employers so that no colored man or woman will be dismissed merely because of race.

These three aspects of the colored man's labor problem are worthy of careful study. They go to the root of the most perplexing immediate phase of what is called the race problem. It is economic equality that gets the emphasis in the speeches and the writings of the colored people themselves. They hate Jim Crow cars and lynching and all acts of race discrimination, in part, because back of these is the big fact that, even in the north, in many skilled occupations, as well as in many unskilled, it is useless for any colored man or woman to ask a job. And so, from year to year, we find the organizations of colored people checking up, listing the new occupations they have entered, pointing to new doors opening to men on the basis of ability where color does not count one way or the other.

The new doors of opportunity opening in Chicago in the last two years, are told here:

Molders. Every foundry in Chicago, according to the Urban league employment office, which chiefly handles the labor situation for colored people, is ready to hire colored molders, who have no difficulty in getting jobs.

Tanneries have opened their doors to both skilled and semi-skilled colored workers.

Colored shipping clerks have entered freight warehouses. Such a statement might seem to have little significance. As in all these instances, however, it is the record of a new precedent. A door once inscribed, "No hope," now says, "There is hope."

Automobile repair shops now employ colored mechanics. The two largest taxi companies make no discrimination on account of color.

One large mattress factory has opened the doors to colored workers.

At the Central Soldiers' and Sailors' bureau at 120 West Adams street, are available for employment colored men who served with the 8th infantry regiment in the Argonne and the St. Mihiel sectors in front line action. There are fifty chauffeurs, twenty first and second cooks, thirty miscellaneous kitchen helpers, five valets and ten butlers of experience, five shipping clerks, five actors, five sales clerks, two stationary engineers, two firemen, two night watchmen and five elevator men.

According to Sergt. H. J. Cannasius, in charge of the division dealing with colored labor, a considerable proportion of the men are justified in refusing to take jobs at heavy labor. "These men were gassed or otherwise wounded in service in the Argonne or in the St. Mihiel actions," he said. "We sent one who had been gassed to take a job as porter in a shoe store in State street. He was in a basement trying to handle a big box of goods. This was the first approach to heavy work he had tackled since he was mustered out. He keeled over, and was taken to a hospital, and it was four days before the doctors would let him go.

"Men who were gassed in France we find are sensitive to dust or fumes. We tried a number in the cement works at Buffington, Ind., but they all came back after a few days. At coal shoveling and at work in coke and coal at gas houses or around vats and retorts where there are fumes these men can't stand up to the work. They come back almost with tears, saying they tried to hold out, but couldn't.

"The Northwestern railroad dining car service has employed a number of ex-soldiers as waiters. Some restaurants and hotels have taken porters and pantrymen at $11 a week and board. We would have no trouble filling calls for more workers in this field. A call came to-day for a colored bookkeeper to go to a normal school at Elizabeth, N.C.

"Some of the returned men of the 8th infantry went to see about getting places as sleeping car porters. They found they would have to stand an initial fee of $35 for uniforms, and as they had no money they gave it up.

"Three of our applicants can fill positions as interpreters or secretaries who are required to know the chief South American and European languages. It is noticeable that some whose homes are in the south say they are going to stay in Chicago, and under no consideration will they go back to Mississippi, Georgia and other states that draw the color line hard and fast. We have five or six applicants a day, new ones, coming in and saying they have chosen the north to live in. They pound on my table and say, "I'll be stiff as this table before I go back south."

Sergt. Cannasius told the story of Edward Burke, of 3632 Vincennes avenue. Burke volunteered for naval service in California before the draft and became chief commissary steward on the ship Mauben. He was discharged at Norfolk and took the best position he could get, that of first cook on a dining car. English, French, German, Italian, Spanish, Portuguese—practically all languages spoken in South America or in central or western Europe—are fluently spoken by Burke. His aspirations are toward a position as interpreter or secretary, but thus far destiny bids him fry eggs and stew beef with his many languages.

The Chicago Whip, a new weekly newspaper, voices

appreciation of two utility corporations that have opened the doors of employment to colored men.

The Peoples Gas company breaks precedent by employing four meter inspectors at salaries of $100 per month and four special meter readers who are boys, 16 years old, at salaries of $55 per month," says the paper. "The experiment of the gas company proved so successful that the Commonwealth Edison company immediately followed suit by placing six colored men in the meter installation department."

[VII]

AFTER EACH LYNCHING

CHICAGO is a receiving station that connects directly with every town or city where the people conduct a lynching.

"Every time a lynching takes place in a community down south you can depend on it that colored people from that community will arrive in Chicago inside of two weeks," says Secretary Arnold Hill of the Chicago Urban league, 3032 South Wabash avenue. "We have seen it happen so often that now whenever we read newspaper dispatches of a public hanging or burning in Texas or a Mississippi town, we get ready to extend greetings to people from the immediate vicinity of the scene of the lynching. If it is Arkansas or Georgia, where a series of lynchings is going on this week, then you may reckon with certainty that there will be large representations from those states among the colored folks getting off the trains at the Illinois Central station two or three weeks from to-day."

Better jobs, the right to vote and have the vote counted at elections, no Jim Crow cars, less race discrimination and a more tolerant attitude on the part of the whites, equal rights with white people in education—these are among the attractions that keep up the steady movement of colored people from southern districts to the north.

"Opportunity, not alms," is the slogan of the educated, while the same thought comes over and over again from the illiterate in their letters, saying, "All we want is a chanst," or, as one spells it, "Let me have a chanch, please."

Hundreds of letters written to The Chicago Defender, the newspaper, and to the Urban league reflect the causes of the migration. Charles Johnston, an investigator for the Carnegie foundation, a lieutenant from overseas with the 803d infantry, believes the economic motive is foremost. He says:

"There are several ways of arriving at a conclusion regarding the economic forces behind the movement of the colored race northward. The factors might be determined by the amount of unemployment or the extent of poverty. These facts are important, but may or may not account for individual action.

"Except in a few localities of the south there was no actual misery or starvation. Nor is it evident that those who left would have perished from want had they remained. Large numbers of negroes have frequently moved around from state to state and even within the states of the south in search of more remunerative employment. The migrations to Arkansas and Oklahoma were expressions of the economic force.

"A striking feature of the northern migration was its individualism. Motives prompting the thousands of negroes were not always the same, not even in the case of close neighbors. The economic motive was foremost, a desire simply to improve their living standards when opportunity beckoned. A movement to the west or even about the south could have proceeded from the same cause.

"Some of the letters reveal a praiseworthy solicitude for their families on the part of the writers. Other letters are an index to poverty and helplessness of home communities.

"In this type of migration the old order is strangely reversed. Instead of leaving an overdeveloped and overcrowded country for undeveloped new territory, they have left the south, backward as it is in development of its resources, for the highly industrialized north. Out of letters from the south we listed seventy-nine different occupations among 1,000 persons asking for information and aid. Property holders, impecunious adventurers, tradesmen, entire labor unions, business and professional men, families, boys and girls, all registered their protests, mildly but determinately, against their homes and sought to move."

From Pensacola, Fla., in May, 1917, came a letter saying, "Would you please let me know what is the price of boarding and rooming in Chicago and where is the best place to get a job before the draft will work? I would rather join the army 1,000 times up there than to join it once down here."

"What I want to say is I am coming north," wrote

another, "and thought I would write you and list a few of the things I can do and see if you can find a place for me anywhere north of the Mason and Dixon line, and I will present myself in person at your office as soon as I hear from you. I am now employed in the R. R. shops at Memphis. I am an engine watchman, hostler, rod cup man, pipe fitter, oil house man, shipping clerk, telephone lineman, freight caller, an expert soaking vat man who can make dope for packing hot boxes on engines. I am capable of giving satisfaction in either of the above-named positions."

"I wish very much to come north," wrote a New Orleans man. "Anywhere in Illinois will do if I am away from the lynchmen's noose and the torchmen's fire. We are firemen, machinist helpers, practical painters and general laborers. And most of all, ministers of the gospel who are not afraid of labor, for it put us where we are."

"I want to ask you for information as to what steps I should take to secure a good position as a first class automobeal blacksmith or any kind pertaining to such," is an inquiry from a large Georgia city. "I have been operating a first class white shop here for quite a number of years, and if I must say, the only colored man in the city that does. Any charges, why notify me, but do not publish my name."

"Please don't publish this in any paper," and "I would not like for my name to be published in the paper," are requests that accompanied two letters from communities where lynchings had occurred.

A girl wrote from Natchez:

"I am writing you to oblige me to put my application in the papers for me, please. I am a body servant or a nice house maid. My hair is black and my eyes are black and I have smooth skin, clear and brown. Good teeth and strong and good health. My weight is 136 lbs."

Here is a sample of the kind of letter that is handed around and talked about down south. It was written by a colored workman in East Chicago, June, 1917, to his former pastor at Union Springs, Ala.:

"It is true the colored men are making good. Pay is never less than $3 per day for ten hours—this not promise. I do not see how they pay such wages the way they work laborers. They do not hurry or drive you. Remember this ($3) is the very lowest wage. Piece work men can make from $6 to $8 a day. They receive their pay every two weeks. I am impressed. My family also. They are doing nicely. I have no right to complain whatever."

"I often think so much of the conversation we used to have concerning this part of the world. I wish many times you could see our people up here, as they are entirely in a different light. I witnessed Decoration day on May 30, the line of march was four miles, eight brass bands. All business houses were closed. I tell you the people here are patriotic. The chief of police dropped dead Friday. Buried him to-day, the procession about three miles long. People are coming here every day and find employment. Nothing here but money, and it is not hard to get. Oh, I have children in school every day with the white children."

Enterprise must be the first name of another who wrote back to Georgia:

"You can hardly get a place to live in here. I am wide awake on my financial plans. I have rented me a place for boarders. I have fifteen sleepers, I began one week ago. I am going into some kind of business here soon.

"The colored people are making good. They are the best workers. I have made a great many white friends. The church is crowded with Baptists from Alabama and Georgia. Ten and twelve join every Sunday. He is planning to build a fine brick church. He takes up 50 and 60 dollars each Sunday."

It must be noted that all the foregoing letters were written with no intent of publication and with no view at all of explaining race migration or factors in housing, employment and education.

[VIII]

TRADES FOR COLORED WOMEN

A COLORED woman entered the office of a north side establishment where artificial flowers are manufactured.

"I have a daughter 17 years old," she said to the proprietor.

"All places filled now," he answered.

"I don't ask a job for her," came the mother's reply. "I want her to learn how to do the work like the white girls do. She'll work for nothing. We don't ask wages, just so she can learn."

So it was arranged for the girl to go to work. Soon she was skilled and drawing wages with the highest in the shop. Other colored girls came in. And now the entire group of fifteen girls that worked in this north side shop have been transferred to a new factory on the south side, near their homes. At the same time a number of colored girls have gone into home work in making artificial flowers.

Such are the casual, hit-or-miss incidents by which the way was opened for colored working people to enter one industry on the same terms as the white wage earners.

Doll hats, lamp shades, millinery—these are three

branches of manufacture where colored labor has entered factories and has also begun home work. Colored workers, with their bundles of finished goods on which the entire family has worked, going to the contractor to turn in the day's output are now a familiar sight in some neighborhoods. In one residence a colored woman employs seven girls, who come to the house every day and make lamp shades, which are later delivered to a contractor. The first week in July thirty girls were placed in one millinery shop.

A notable recent development, partly incidental to conditions of war industry, is the entrance of colored women into garment factories, particularly where women's and children's garments are made. In Chicago in the last year they have been assigned to the operation of power machines making children's clothes, women's apparel, overalls and rompers.

Out of 170 firms in Chicago that employed colored women for the first time during the war, 42, or 24 per cent, were hotels or restaurants, which hired them as kitchen help or bus girls. Twenty-one, or 12 per cent, were hotels or apartment houses which hired them as chambermaids. Nineteen laundries, 12 garment-factories, seven stores, and eight firms, hiring laborers and janitresses, make up the rest of the 170. The packing industry, of course, leads all others in employment of both colored men and women as workers. Occupations that engaged still others during the war were picture framers, capsule makers, candy wrappers, tobacco strippers, noodle makers, nut shellers, furniture sand-paperers, corset repairers, paper box makers, ice cream cone strippers, poultry dressers and bucket makers.

In a building near the public library is a colored woman who conducts a hair-dressing parlor. She employs three white girls. All the patrons are white. The proprietress herself could easily pass for a Brazilian banana planter's widow, of Spanish Caucasian blood. But as she frankly admits that she is one-eighth African and seven-eighths Caucasian, she has been refused admission to other buildings when she wished for various reasons to change the location of her establishment.

Here and there, slowly and by degrees, the line of color discrimination breaks. A large chain of dairy lunchrooms in Chicago employs colored bus girls, cooks and dishwashers and depends almost entirely on colored help to do the rougher work.

More notable yet is the fact that a downtown business college informs employment bureaus that it is able to place any and all colored graduates of the college in positions as stenographers and typists. In a few loop stores colored salesgirls are employed. In one shoe store beginning this policy, a white girl filed complaint. The manager investigated and found there was no objection except from this one white girl, who was thereupon dismissed.

A mattress factory opened wage earning opportunities to colored women in the last year. Two taxicab companies now hire women as cleaners. The foregoing list

of occupations just about completes the recital of progress in this regard in Chicago in the last year.

Colored women were occupied during the war in
various cities in making soldiers' uniforms, horses'
gas masks, belts, puttees, leggings, razor blade cases,
gloves, veils, embroideries, raincoats, books, cigars, cig-
arettes, dyed furs, millinery, candy, artificial feathers,
buttons, toys, marabou and women's garments.

The comment of a trained industrial observer on the
colored woman as a machine operator is as follows:

"Few as yet are skilled as machine or hand operators.
Because of their newness to industrial work, the major-
ity have been put on processes requiring no training and
small manual ability. They are employed at repetitive
hand operations, and occasionally run a foot press or
a power sewing machine. In one millinery shop, however, the superintendent said that every colored worker
in his shop preferred machine operation to hand work.

"Replacement for colored women, however, does not
mean advancement in the same sense as for white
women. Because the white woman has been in industry
for a long time, and is more familiar with industrial
practices, she is less willing to accept bad working conditions. The colored woman, on the other hand, is hand-
icapped by industrial ignorance and drifts into conditions of work rejected by white workers. Colored
women are found on processes white women refuse to
perform. They replace boys and men at cleaning win-
dow shades, dyeing furs, and in one factory they were

found bending constantly and lifting clumsy 160 pound bales of material.

"Inquiries as to the general attitude of white workers toward the introduction of colored women brought conflicting reports. About half the employers claimed that their white workers had no objection to the colored women; that they were either cordial or entirely indifferent toward them. Of the other half, some said their white workers objected when the colored workers were first hired, but felt no prejudice now. Other white workers preferred to have the two groups segregated. Still others were willing to let the colored workers do unskilled work, but refused to allow them on the skilled processes.

"At the time of the greatest labor shortage in the history of this country, colored women were the last to be employed. They did the most menial and by far the most underpaid work. They were the marginal workers all through the war, and yet during those perilous times, the colored woman made just as genuine a contribution to the cause of democracy as her white sister in the munitions factory or her brother in the trench. She released the white women for more skilled work and she replaced colored men who went into service."

The report of a study jointly directed by representatives of the Consumers' league, Y.M.C.A., Y.W.C.A., Russell Sage foundation and other organizations recommends that greater emphasis be placed on the training of the colored girl by more general education and more trade training through apprenticeship and trade schools, and also that every effort be made to stimulate trade organizations among colored women by education of colored women working toward organization, education of colored workers for industrial leadership and keener understanding of colored women in industry among organized and unorganized white workers. And, lastly, an appreciation and acceptance of the colored woman in industry by the American employer and the public at large is urged.

A creed of cleanliness was issued in thousands of copies by the Chicago Urban league during the big influx of colored people from the south. It recognized that the woman, always the woman is finally responsible for the looks and upkeep of a household, and made its appeal in the following language:

"For me! I am an American citizen. I am proud of our boys 'over there,' who have contributed soldier service. I desire to render citizen service. I realize that our soldiers have learned new habits of self-respect and cleanliness. I desire to help bring about a new order of living in this community. I will attend to the neatness of my personal appearance on the street or when sitting in the front doorway. I will refrain from wearing dustcaps, bungalow aprons, house clothing and bedroom shoes when out of doors. I will arrange my toilet within doors and not on the front porch. I will insist upon the use of rear entrances for coal dealers and hucksters. I will refrain from loud talking and objectionable deportment on street cars and in public places. I will do my best to prevent defacement of property, either by children or adults."

Two photographs went with this creed. One showed an unclean, messy front porch, the other a clean, well kept front porch. Such is the propaganda of order and decency carried on earnestly and ceaselessly by clubs, churches and leagues of colored people, struggling to bring along the backward ones of a people whose heritage is 200 years of slavery and fifty years of industrial boycott.

As an aside from the factual and the humdrum of the foregoing, here is a letter, vivid with roads and by-paths of spiritual life, written by a colored woman to her sister in Mississippi. It is a frank confession of one sister soul to another of what life has brought, and as a document is worth more than stacks of statistics.

"My Dear Sister:—I was agreeably surprised to hear from you and to hear from home. I am well and thankful to say I am doing well. The weather and everything else was a surprise to me when I came. I got here in time to attend one of the greatest revivals in the history of my life. Over 500 people joined the church. We had a Holy Ghost shower. You know I like to have run wild. It was snowing some nights and if you didn't hurry you could not get standing room.

"Please remember me kindly to any who ask of me. The people are rushing here by the thousands, and I know if you come and rent a big house you can get all the roomers you want. You write me exactly when you are coming. I am not keeping house. I am living with my brother and his wife. My son is in California, but will be home soon. He spends his winter in California. I can get a nice place for you to stop until you can look around and see what you want.

"I am quite busy. I work for a packing company in the sausage department. My daughter and I work in the same department. We get $1.50 a day and we pack so many sausages we don't have much time to play, but it is a matter of a dollar with me and I feel that God made the path and I am walking therein.

"Tell your husband work is plentiful here and he won't have to loaf if he wants to work. I know unless old man A—— changed it was awful with his soul. Well, I guess I have said about enough. I will be delighted to look into your face once more in life. Pray for me, for I am heaven bound. I have made too many rounds to slip now. I know you will pray for me, for prayer is the life of any sensible man or woman. Good-by."

[IX]

NEGROES AND RISING RENTS

ONE of the best known club women in Chicago sold an apartment house on Wabash avenue last month. It cost her $26,000. She sold it for $14,000. Her agent advised her to make the sale because, as he said, the colored people were coming into the neighborhood and the property surely was going to take a slump.

That is Chapter I of the little story. Chapter II opens with the rent of each apartment taking a jump from $35 to $50 in this identical apartment house that had apparently taken such a drop in value in the open market. The fact is that it wasn't an open market. It was a panicky market. Sold openly, so that all prospective buyers might have had opportunity to bid, the place would have brought a higher price than was originally paid for it.

In two other instances in this same neighborhood properties at one time worth $15,000 dropped to $8,-000 and $6,000, respectively, in a market so managed that there was no competitive bidding. The sellers were filled with panic. Then the rents took a high jump after the sales were made.

There seem to be certain preposterous axioms of

real estate exchange governing this district and no others in Chicago. These axioms might be stated thus: (1) Sell at a loss and the rent goes higher, and (2) the larger the number of colored persons ready to pay higher rentals, the lower the realty values slump.

To quote a paragraph from the housing survey of the school of civics and philanthropy:

"It is a matter of common knowledge that house after house, flat after flat, whether under white or black agents, comes to the negro at an increased rental. The only available argument, it would seem, which will ever dispel the public impressions is for instances to become just as numerous of charge downward as they now are of charge upward. A negro woman, recent purchaser of a modern six flat building on the south side, informed the investigator that she had been importuned by numerous white agents and by two negro dealers, one of whom she named, to allow them to rent her flat for her at a substantial increase above the rent she is now receiving, acting as her own agent."

The report says further: "Counter-charges are made against the negro tenant by dealers of both races." It considers these charges in extensive detail, and then declares:

"It is established that, despite the low rents, which are immaterial in the light of circumstances, the general housing condition of negroes in the area lying between State street and the railroad tracks, stretching for several blocks north and south of 27th street, is reprehensible, a menace to health and constitutes kindling wood sufficient to keep Chicago in constant danger of disastrous conflagration.

"Whatever may be the contributing causes, demand and supply, overbidding for coveted places on the part of tenants, inconspicuousness of the negro as an economic factor, guaranteed rentals or what not, the negro in Chicago, paid a lower wage than the white workman and more limited in opportunity, does pay a relatively higher rent. The negro real estate man is much fairer, generally speaking, than is supposed, and could means be found whereby he and the tenant could get together and come to an understanding on many things, each about the other, regarding which they are now deluded, the first step would have been taken to the improvement of the lot of the negro renter."

Twenty years ago fewer than fifty families of the colored race were home owners in Chicago. To-day they number thousands, their purchases ranging from $200 to $20,000, from tar paper shacks in the steel district to brownstone and graystone establishments with wealthy or well to do white neighbors. In most cases, where a colored man has investments of more than ordinary size, it is in large part in real estate. Realty investment and management seem to be an important field of operation among those colored people who acquire substance.

In the matter of home buying there is something radically abnormal about the situation of the colored people in Chicago. The last census computed 22.5 per cent of the homes occupied by colored citizens in the United States as owned by the occupants. In Illinois 23 per cent of the colored householders owned their premises. But in Chicago the survey of the school of civics and philanthropy in 1917 reported that in the south division only 4 per cent of the apartments and houses occupied by colored persons were owned by the occupants and on the west side only 8 per cent. In South Chicago and in the stockyards district, where the highest percentage of ownership was found, 18 per cent of the colored families owned their homes. So it is evident that the percentage of home owners in the district around 35th and State streets is desperately low as compared with other Chicago districts and as compared with the country at large.

It is easy to understand how the doubling of population during the late war made a live real estate situation. Not only was it difficult for the newcomers to buy homes, if they so desired, but it was hard at times for them even to get a place to sleep. The Urban league canvassed real estate dealers one day and found 664 colored applicants for houses on that day and only fifty supplied. The demands for quarters, the higher rentals paid by colored people and other factors were responsible for thirty-six new localities being opened up within three months, these localities having formerly been exclusively white. This increase in rents was from 5 to 30 per cent, and in a few cases 50 per cent.

"To-day we are beginning to realize that to become a good citizen, it is necessary to own a home, and that those who are renting cannot be considered other than floaters," is the comment of Jesse Binga, banker, the oldest established colored real estate dealer in Chicago.

When Binga bought one corner on South State street it was valued at $300 a front foot. It is now worth $500 a front foot. Six saloons did a fast business in that neighborhood when he entered there, and it was said of it, "You could get anything you wanted, from a footrace to a murder." Now it is a quiet, ordinary residence corner, and in behavior and cleanliness it ranks as one of the best in Chicago.

Though there are 249 building and loan associations in Chicago, there was none for the colored race until the Pyramid Building and Loan association, financed and officered by colored men, came into existence this year. There have been 690 shares sold to 105 persons.

Housing surveys of colored residence districts, varying in scope and purposes, are being conducted by the Cook county real estate board and the city public welfare department. One of the best publications on this subject is a pamphlet by Lieut. Charles S. Duke, a colored man, a Harvard graduate, and an engineer in the bridge division of the public works department at the city hall. It was published last April and it summarizes proposals for immediate action under two heads.

First are "things that Chicago owes her colored citizens," which are stated as follows:

1. The privilege of borrowing money easily upon real estate occupied by colored citizens living on the south side, and in the same amounts as can be borrowed upon property located in other parts of the city.

2. Better attention in the matter of repairs and upkeep of premises occupied by colored tenants.

3. Making an end of the neglect of neighborhoods occupied principally by colored people.

·4. Abandonment of all attempts at racial segregation.

5. Prohibition, as far as possible, of the commercializing of race prejudice in real estate matters.

6. Recovery from hysteria incident to the advent of the first colored neighbors.

7. Fewer indignation meetings and more constructive planning.

8. Better school houses and more modern equipment in schools in districts where colored people live in large numbers.

9. More playgrounds and recreational centers on the south side.

10. A beautiful branch library in the center of the colored district.

As a corollary are presented these "things that colored citizens owe Chicago":

1. Better care of premises occupied by them, either as tenants or as landlords.

2. Formation of improvement clubs for the beautification of the neighborhoods in which they may live.

3. Practice of thrift and economy in the spending of income.

4. Keeping the expenditures within the income.

5. The buying of beautiful, sanitary homes.

6. Spending less money for amusements and expensive clothing.

7. Checkmating of the real estate broker who makes it his business to capitalize race prejudice in his dealings.

8. Reduction of the lodger evil.

9. Ending of the practice of taking on real estate obligations beyond the purchaser's means.

10. A continual demand for all the civic benefits that a beautiful and progressive city like Chicago can confer upon its citizens.

[X]

UNIONS AND THE COLOR LINE

AT the Saddle and Sirloin club there sat in conference one day a few months ago representatives from
two groups. On one side of the table were men speaking
for the most active organizations of colored people in
Chicago in matters of employment and general welfare.
On the other side of the table were men speaking for the
packers who employ at the stockyards upwards of
15,000 colored men and women, interests that are to-day
and are expected to be in the future the largest employers of colored labor.

Four points to constitute a guiding policy in employment were offered by the colored representatives, with
a statement that the principles embodied the general
sense of the leaders of social, industrial, welfare and
religious groups of the colored race in Chicago. After
discussion the representatives of the packers agreed to
accept the four points, and they are regarded by the colored people as in force and effective until further notice.

The four points as phrased in the conference at the
Saddle and Sirloin club, are:

1. That whenever we are attempting to introduce
negro workers into trades in which white workers are

unionized, we must urge the negroes to join the unions.

2. That when we are introducing negro labor into industries in which the white workers are not unionized, we advise negroes, in case the effort is made to unionize the industry, to join with their white comrades.

3. That we strongly urge the organizers of all the unions in industries which may be opened to colored labor, not only to permit, but actively to assist in incorporating negroes into the unions.

4. In cases where negroes are prevented from joining the unions, the right is reserved of complete liberty of action as to the advice that will be given to negro working men.

With these points in force, the men concerned felt that they had taken all steps humanly possible to avert any such disaster as came to East St. Louis, where labor conditions were a factor.

Estimates as to the number of colored workers who have joined the trade unions of the Stockyards Labor council vary from 6,000 to 10,000. The organizers say they are too busy to make even an approximate count. They say further that the organizations are mixed colored and white, and a count of membership is not as easy as it would be if all colored members were segregated in one local. Such a segregation is not being thought of.

"Men who work together in mixed gangs of white and colored workers believe their trade union ought to be organized just like the work gang," said A. K.

Foote, a colored man whose craft is that of hog killer and who is secretary of local 651 of the Amalgamated Meat Cutters and Butcher Workmen of North America.

"If you ask me what I think about race prejudice, and whether it's getting better," he said, "I'll tell you the one place in this town where I feel safest is over at the yards, with my union button on. The union is for protection, that's our cry. We put that on our organization wagons and trucks traveling the stockyards district, in signs telling the white and colored men that their interests are identical.

"We had a union ball a while ago in the Coliseum annex, and 2,000 people were there. The whites danced with their partners and the colored folks with theirs. The hog butchers' local gave a picnic recently and they came around to our people with tickets to sell, and the attendance at the picnic was cosmopolitan. Whenever you hear any of that race riot stuff, you can be sure it is not going to start around here. Here they are learning that it pays for white and colored men to call each other brother."

Local 651 has a commodious, well-kept office at 43d and State streets. It is known as the "miscellaneous" local, taking in as members the common laborers and all workers not qualifying for membership in a skilled craft union. One advantage for colored workers, according to organizers, is that the seniority rights of such workers are now accorded. If the head of a work gang quits for any reason and a colored man is the oldest in point of service in the gang or department, he is automatically advanced. When an organization meeting was held recently on a Sunday afternoon in a public school yard at 33d street and Wentworth avenue, the police directed that the parade of the colored workmen from their hall at 43d and State streets must not march down State street through the district most heavily populated with negroes. The union officials are still mystified by the police explanation that it was safer and better for the colored procession to take a line of march where there were the smallest number of negro residents on the streets.

Margaret Bondfield, fraternal delegate from the British trades union congress, spoke to the audience, which numbered about 3,000. Probably 2,000 stood in the hot sun three hours while the American Giants (colored) played in the next lot, and the White Sox game was on only two blocks away.

John Riley and C. Ford, organizers carrying authorizations from the American Federation of Labor, were speakers. Ford has personality, rides rough-shod over English grammar, but wins his crowd with homely points such as these:

"If I had any prejudice against a white man in this crowd any more than I've got against a colored man, then I'd jump down here off this platform and break my infernal neck right now."

"You boys know about rassling. You know if you throw a rassler down you know you got to stay down with him if you're going to keep him down: If you don't stay down with him, he'll get up and you got to throw him again."

"You notice there ain't no Jim Crow cars here to-day. That's what organization does. The truth is there ain't no negro problem any more than there's a Irish problem or a Russian or a Polish or a Jewish or any other problem. There is only the human problem, that's all. All we demand is the open door. You give us that, and we won't ask nothin' more of you."

It was a curious equation of human races that stood listening to this talk. Lithuanians, Poles, Slovaks, Italians and colored men mingled in all sections of the crowd, and every speaker touching the topic of prejudice got the same kind of a response from all parts of the crowd. So they stood in the July afternoon sun, listening as best they could to what they could hear from their orators, while the noisy cheers and laughter of two ball games came on the air in great gusts. They were 2,000 men for whom the race problem is solved. Their theory is that when economic equality of the races is admitted, then the social, housing, real estate, transportation or educational phases are not difficult.

"We all know there are unions in the American Federation of Labor that have their feet in the 20th century and their heads in the 16th century," said Secretary Johnstone of the Stockyards Labor council, as applause swept the sunburned 2,000. He was referring to the unions that draw the color line.

The Rev. L. K. Williams of Olivet Baptist church, which has a membership of 8,500, and the Rev. John F. Thomas of the Ebenezer Baptist church at 35th and Dearborn streets, besides other clergymen, have voiced approval of the campaign for organization of colored labor in affiliation with the trade union movement. There was dissent to organization spoken by a few ministers at one time, but this is said now to have changed to approval.

A unique memorial was circulated among all colored clergymen in Chicago by five labor unions in which the colored people have a large representation. In order that each copy should bear proof of its authenticity, it was embossed with the seal of each of the five unions and signed by the officers. The memorial read:

"Whereas, God is the creator of all mankind and has endowed us with certain inalienable rights that should be respected one by the other, so that peace and harmony will reign and hell on earth be subdued; and,

"Whereas, the unscrupulous white plutocrats, aided by corrupt politicians, have usurped even the rights of the workers guaranteed by the constitution and supplanted oppression and discord by propagating race hatred, discrimination and class distinction, and

"Whereas, the credulous common people (white and black) have been the maltreated tools of these financial master mechanics, and their fallacious teachings have kept us divided and made their throne more secure, and

"Whereas, the power of the united front and concerted action of all toilers is the only medium through which industrial and political democracy can be obtained, wage slavery and unjust legislation destroyed, and

"Whereas, the executive board of the American Federation of Labor on April 22, 1918, in Washington, D.C., was met by a committee of recognized race leaders, and adopted plans thoroughly to organize the colored workers in industry, putting them on the same economic level with other races; therefore, be it

"Resolved, that we appeal to the conscientious race leaders, intellectuals and other God fearing men of influence, who believe in human rights, justice and fair play and are desirous of conveying light and plenty where darkness and want predominate, to assist the 60,000 colored members of the American Federation of Labor in fostering and encouraging members of our race to affiliate with the bona fide labor movement, to the end that we will have a larger representation in this industrial army, which will exemplify to the white progressives, as well as autocrats, that we are 'straws in the new broom of reconstruction, that will sweep clean American institutions, ridding them of discrimination and corruption.' "

With the official union seals were the signatures of George A. Swan, president; Hugh Swift, vice president, and R. E. Copeland, secretary of the Musicians' Protective union; Garrett Rice, president, A. L. Johnson, vice president, and A. Welcher, secretary of the Railway Coach Cleaners' union; N. S. Wimms, president, and P. D. Campbell, vice president, of the Sleeping Car Porters of America; Annie M. Jones, president, Isabel Case, vice president, and Mabel Kinglin, secretary of local 213 of the Butcher Workmen's union; Henry Pappers, president, J. W. Smith, vice president, and A. K. Foote, secretary of local 651 of the Butcher Workmen's union.

There is odd humor in the fact that Dr. George C. Hall, a colored surgeon and real estate proprietor to the extent of $100,000, has been for years an honorary member of the Meat Cutters' and Butcher Workmen's union. Dr. Hall always has contended that organization is one route away from race discrimination.

[XI]

ABOUT LYNCHINGS

"ELEVEN persons joined our church the other Sunday and they were all from Vicksburg, Miss., where there had been a lynching a few weeks before," said Dr. L. K. Williams, colored pastor of the largest protestant church in North America, in an address to the Baptist Ministers' council of Chicago.

Tuskeegee institute records of lynchings the first six months of this year show the following numbers in the states named: Alabama, 3; Arkansas, 4; Florida, 2; Georgia, 3; Louisiana, 4; Mississippi, 7; Missouri, 1; North Carolina, 2; South Carolina, 1; Texas, 1. The total, 28, is seven less than in the corresponding period of 1918 and fourteen more than in the corresponding period of 1917.

Not only is Chicago a receiving station and port of refuge for colored people who are anxious to be free from the jurisdiction of lynch law, but there has been built here a publicity or propaganda machine that directs its appeals or carries on an agitation that every week reaches hundreds of thousands of people of the colored race in the southern states. The State street blocks south of 31st street are a "newspaper row," with the Defender, the Broad Ax, the Plaindealer, the Searchlight, the Guide, the Advocate, the Whip, as weekly publications, and there are also illustrated monthly magazines such as the Half Century and the Favorite.

The Defender is the dean of the weekly newspaper group, and it is said to reach more than 100,000 subscribers in southern states. A Carnegie foundation investigator records his belief that the Defender, more than any other one agency, was the cause of the "northern fever" and the big exodus from the south in the last three years. It advocates race pride and race militancy and exhausted the vocabulary of denunciation on lynching, disfranchisement, and all forms of race discrimination.

At some postoffices in the south it was difficult to have copies of the Defender delivered to subscribers. A colored man caught with a copy in his possession was suspected of "northern fever" and other so-called disloyalties. Thousands of letters poured into the Defender office asking about conditions in the north.

This situation had a curious political reflex. A rumor arose. It traveled to Chicago and Washington. It said that sinister forces were operating to prevent negroes in the north and particularly in Chicago from returning to their former homes in the south. Down south the rumor traveled and was published to the effect that thousands of colored men and women were walking the streets of

Chicago, hungry and without shoes, begging for transportation to Dixie, the home of the cotton blossoms
that they were longing to see again.

Lieut. W. L. Owen of the military intelligence service at Washington was sent to Chicago to investigate.
He went to Dr. George C. Hall, a leader in several
colored organizations, and asked, "What is this undercurrent that is keeping the negroes in the north?" Dr.
Hall answered, "There isn't any undercurrent. Everything is in the open in this case. The trouble started
when the Declaration of Independence was written. It
says that every man has a right to life, liberty and the
pursuit of happiness. So long as the colored people get
more of those three things in the north than in the south
they are going to keep coming, and they are going to
stay."

Dr. Hall told the intelligence officer that the situation
reminded him of the reply of the colored band leader
to Liza Johnson, who asked what was the occasion of
the brass band's parading the streets one evening. The
reply was, "Lordy, Liza, don't you know we don't need
no occasion?"

The declaration of Dr. Williams to the Baptist Ministers' association that eleven new members came from
Vicksburg has a direct connection with a lynching story
which is being widely circulated by the publicity or
propaganda batteries of South State street, reaching at
least 1,000,000 of the illiterate colored people of the
south. The story, for ingenious cruelty and with relation

to the kind of barbarism that is worse for the practitioners than the victims, equals anything recited in recent European war atrocities or anything in the Spanish inquisition of more ancient days.

In Vicksburg, in the third week in June, the story goes, a colored man accused of an assault on a white woman was placed in a hole that came to his shoulders. Earth was tamped around his neck, only his head being left above ground. A steel cage five feet square then was put over the head of the victim and a bulldog was put inside the cage. Around the dog's head was tied a paper bag filled with red pepper to inflame his nostrils and eyes. The dog immediately lunged at the victim's head. Further details are too gruesome to print.

Whatever may be the truth about this amazing story, it is published in newspapers of the colored people and is attested as a fact by Secretary A. Clement McNeal of the National Association for the Advancement of Colored People, whose local office is at 3333 South State street.

The last named organization, the most militant in activities against lynching, will hold its annual convention next year for the first time in a southern city. It will go to Atlanta on invitation of the mayor of that city and on request of Gov. Dorsey of Georgia. This is one of several indications that the southern states are actively considering steps to be taken to retain their negro population and to lessen the violence which threatens to become a habit in a number of communities.

[XII]

NEGRO CRIME TALES

OUTBREAKS of race warfare reported from Washington, D.C., cause leaders of the colored people in Chicago to place emphasis on two points. (1) That Washington has had a large inflow of southern white population during recent years, while the regular army is known to have a larger proportion of whites from the southern states than from any other section; (2) that the reported clashes may be something else than racial hostilities and, perhaps, may be traced back to the same antagonisms as those which caused the sectional war from 1860 to 1865.

John Hawkins, formerly with the federal department of justice and more recently in the second deputy superintendent's office of the Chicago police department, gives this view:

"The newspaper reports of what is happening in Washington have most frequently indicated that the causes of the outbreaks were attacks by colored soldiers on white women. Though this is a serious and sinister charge to repeat day after day in dispatches that go to the entire nation, the fact is that there have been no supporting details, no particulars of knowledge or information such as any court of law or any intelligent person requires before arriving at an opinion or a conviction.

"In one instance a dispatch contained the following three sentences: 'Even while the rioting was at its height early to-day reports of another attack upon a white woman came. Frightened away once, her assailant hid and seized her as she left her house. She escaped only when all but stripped of her clothing.'

"Here we have the gravest sort of a charge. No names are given, no locations, no witnesses—a wild inflammatory tale sent out on the swift wings of rumor and gabbled and tattled for the consumption of a nation of people struggling to set an example to the rest of the world on the value of self control during a great world crisis.

"In all cases where the old and familiar statement is made that 'a negro attacked a white woman,' let there be something more than this vague allegation. It has too often served to screen ulterior purposes. Unless such a statement is accompanied by names, dates and locations, and has at least a semblance of such facts as are required when a white man is similarly involved, it should be assumed that the vague allegations are camouflage behind which men are working to defeat the intent of the emancipation proclamation, men who hold to the feudal south's theory that the negro is biologically inferior to the white man."

The Anti-Vilification society has been organized by

colored men in Chicago who believe that the United States as a republic is headed in the right direction, but that there is being carried on persistent propaganda that can bring no good to the nation. Lieut. Charles S. Duke, colored, a graduate of Harvard university, and Edward H. Morris, an able colored lawyer who is reported to have a fortune close to $1,000,000, are among the officers of the organization.

"A few days ago there was a lynching in a Mississippi town," said Lieut. Duke. "One New Orleans newspaper reported that the victim had confessed, while another newspaper said it was reported that he had confessed to a crime. On so vitally important a matter as whether a man to be burned by a mob had confessed guilt the mediums of public information did not agree."

A committee representing a number of organizations of colored people called on the Illinois state council of defense one day while the late war was on. They carried copies of a front page newspaper story wherein it was stated that at a north shore society event the hostess took particular pains not to shake hands with the members of the colored "jazz" orchestra. The members of the state council of defense recognized that the article was a gratuitous insult to the colored people, and the continuance of such a news policy during the war might seriously affect the colored fighters and workers.

Equality is a big word in the various public movements among the colored people. The following program adopted recently by the National Association for the Advancement of Colored People contains in brief a statement of the kinds of equality they are seeking:

1. A vote for every negro man and woman on the same terms as for white men and women. This is accorded in practically all northern states, but not in the states south of Mason and Dixon's line.

2. An equal chance to acquire the kind of an education that will enable the negro everywhere to use his vote wisely.

3. A fair trial in the courts for all crimes of which he is accused by judges in whose election he has participated, without discrimination because of race.

4. A right to sit upon the jury which passes upon him.

5. Defense against lynching and burning at the hands of mobs.

6. Equal service on railroads and other public carriers, this to mean sleeping car service, dining car service, Pullman service, at the same cost and on the same terms as other passengers.

7. Equal right to the use of public parks, libraries and other community services for which he is taxed.

8. An equal chance for a livelihood in public and private employment.

9. The abolition of color-hyphenation and the substitution of "straight Americanism."

[XIII]

COLORED GAMBLERS

IN South State street, in blocks near 35th street, there are colored men who stand on the sidewalk and pick out faces from the human stream flowing by. They saunter carelessly out and meet these faces and speak words addressed to the ears adjusted behind the faces. These words usually are: "Try your wrist to-day? Try your wrist?"

The immemorial game of craps calls for wrist play. Of course, it is entirely a matter of luck or fate, unless the dice are loaded, but the sidewalk cappers in South State street assume that it takes a skill of the human wrist to throw the requisite sevens and elevens that are necessary to what is technically known as a "killing." So they ask, "Try your wrist?"

"Billy" Lewis for months has been running a place between 3510 and 3512 South State street, called the Pioneer club, where craps and poker are the attractions. The entrance is between two store buildings. A capper is usually in front day and night. From early in the afternoon till far in the morning players dribble in and out of this passageway, usually one customer at a time, occasionally two or three customers together, but generally everything looking quiet and orderly, though the attendance of the Pioneer club in the rear goes as high as seventy-five and 100 men when the "going" is good.

This is not the only craps and poker enterprise conducted by "Billy" Lewis. He has another at 14 East 35th street, where the second and third floors are used as a temple of the gods of chance. Also he has another at 37 West 22d street.

"Louie Joe" presides over craps at a place in the 3000 block on South State street, second floor front. "Mexican Frank" has his establishment at 3436 South State street, second floor front. "Wiley" Coleman is in the same block on South State street, second floor front.

It should be stated here that in most cases the neighboring shops, stores and flat dwellers do not enjoy the proximity of the poker and craps enthusiasts. In every instance where inquiry was made the neighbors said they wished the police would stop the games.

W. M. Bass has been operating craps and poker games night and day in the rear of a real estate office on East 31st street, near Cottage Grove avenue. From an alley entrance at 3512 South State street, one may enter a temple of chance conducted by one McFallin. Two men known as "Williams" and "Kennedy" maintain a laboratory for the study of the laws of chance on South State street, near 35th street, entrances front and rear. T. Jones has a similar laboratory on South State street, near 39th street, second floor, front and rear entrances.

"From 22d street to 39th street on South State street

there is some kind of a game going here and there, usually craps and poker, and often day and night," said an informant who knows the district from constant residence in it and wide acquaintance.

"I'm no reformer," he commented further, "I don't want to have the duty of changing what is in men's natures. But you can take it from me, they're going too far out here now. There ain't many places where the game is square. The workingman who falls for a capper and thinks he is going to try his wrist, he don't try his wrist at all. He goes up against dice that are fixed and cards that are marked and they take his money away from him."

Now for the contrast. Take a look at the buildings where live some of the victims of the gamblers, who are naturally also the victims of the police who let the gamblers run the kind of games that are run.

A house to house canvass was made by a colored newspaper man of two blocks of residences or tenements in Dearborn street adjacent to the South State street craps and poker games. The figures jotted down in the notebook of this investigator have a special significance when it is recalled that it is from these tenements that the gambling houses get part of their customers.

Within two blocks were found a total of eighty-three families where 96 per cent of the boys were truants from the public schools, and 72 per cent of these boys were retarded at least one year by reason of truancy.

In most cases the parents were away from home so much that they were out of touch with the children. At sixty-two homes the condition of furniture, walls and ceilings was classified as "dilapidated." In five instances there was water dripping into a living room from a toilet room in bad order on a floor above.

In thirty-one cases the father had "deserted," which means he is tired, dead, sick or gone wrong from unknown causes. In nineteen cases the father of the family was dead, and the mother was struggling with a variously sized brood of young ones. In twenty-eight cases the father was a heavy drinker. Three of the fathers were in jail and eleven homes were motherless. Forty mothers worked all day, twenty mothers were "heavy drinkers," to use the classification employed by this investigator. Forty-two refused to answer questions.

The following sweeping summary was noted:

"Fifty-one per cent of the cases revealed home broken by death, desertion, divorce, drink, promiscuous living or degeneracy, and cases where the deserted mother was found living in open shame before her children or where a father who is a widower was living in open shame before his children."

Such are fragmentary notes of a district in which a Chicagoan might pick up as many "Broken Blossoms" as Thomas Burke found in one quarter of London.

At the corner of 34th and South State streets the Rev. W. C. Thompson of the Pentecostal Church of Christ ended a street meeting that was rich and vibrant with melody. He explained that the police sometimes run him and his singers off the street, but the meetings would be kept up until the next time the police took such action.

"New things is comin' altogether diverse from what they has been," said this preacher in a rush of eloquence, and twenty voices of men and women shook out irresistible and magnetic melody to a song called "After a While." The last stanza ran like this:

"Our boasted land and nation is plunging in disgrace
With pictures of starvation in almost every place,
While plenty of needed money remains in horrid piles,
But God's going to rule this nation after a while.
    After a while,
    After a while,
God's going to rule this nation, after a while."

[XIV]

AN OFFICIAL OF THE PACKERS

AMONG the employers, executives and superintendents of the packing houses, the clashes between white and colored people in the stockyards and adjacent districts are not a race question so much as a labor union question, according to a prominent official of one of the packing companies.

This official sat in various conferences of yards officials and state, city and militia officers during the days of riot. He is familiar with the views of the officials of the large packing companies and believes that the following expressions represent the general viewpoint of the packers.

"In the yards it is not a race question at all. It is a labor union question. We have no objections to the negroes joining the union. We are running an open shop. The unions want us to run a closed shop. That would mean we could hire only union men. The unions have done everything to get the negro into their membership, but they haven't got him. That is the trouble. At one time, we heard, they had about 90 per cent of all the negroes in the yards in the unions. But they don't stay.

"The trouble is that the negro is not naturally a good union man. He doesn't like to pay union dues.

"We are going to take back into our employ all the negroes who are now away on account of the riots. Just now it is a good thing for those who have gone too far to cool off. If we should close down our plants for two weeks many would realize more clearly what is needed in this hour.

"There has never been any organized effort on our part to bring the negro here. The packers' percentage of increase of negro employes is not greater than that of any other industry during the war. The steel plants, the railroads and others increased about the same percentage we did. High wages was the inducement that drew them north. We expect that the negro will continue to be the chief source of surplus labor. In all our experience there have been no race clashes, no strictly racial trouble, inside of the yards while the men are working. Their work requires skill in the handling of axes, cleavers and knives and if there were any real and lasting race hatred, it would show itself in violence inside the yards where they work.

"At the present time 21 per cent of the workers in one large plant are colored. During the war at the time of highest pressure they numbered from 24 to 25 per cent. Before the war they numbered 18 per cent.

"With the negroes away as at present we are able to operate the plants at only 60 per cent capacity. This lowered production and lessened amount of commodities for the market will have a measurable reflection in prices of food. It also affects the producers of our raw material. The farmer who had a bad experience marketing hogs last week when the shutdown was on because of the riots, may say to himself that hogs are not the best things to raise for market.

"Our plant superintendents say that the white men want the colored workers back on some kinds of work. Take the beef luggers. They carry on their shoulders the quarters of beefs. Negroes have always been best at this."

The following figures represent the distribution of nationalities and race among the employes of Armour & Co.: 2,052 Poles, 2,000 negroes, 1,372 Lithuanians, 5,167 Americans, 141 Bohemians, 118 Jews, 669 Irish, 41 Greeks, 300 Germans, 150 Slovaks, 56 Mexicans, 205 Russians, 23 Scots, 55 Italians.

The employes of the other plants are said to be divided in about the same proportions.

[XV]

MR. JULIUS ROSENWALD
INTERVIEWED

AT Sears, Roebuck & Co., where the volume of business is $200,000,000 a year, where they send out 8,000,000 copies a year of the most widely circulated book in the United States—the Sears, Roebuck & Co. catalogue—there sits in the administration office the president of the company, Julius Rosenwald.

In the midst of an array of wall photographs of Greek parthenons and Egyptian sphinxes there is a large photograph of Booker T. Washington, the negro race leader. Near at hand is a remarkable collection of books on the race question.

"If we say the negro must stay in slums and shall not invade white residence districts, then we shall have to make more stringent health laws to protect us from the evils that go with slums," said Mr. Rosenwald. "If we say the negro must continue to live in slums, we must prepare for a brighter crime rate.

"They came here because we asked them to come, because they were needed for industrial service. There is no solution for the problem apparent now. That is all the more reason both sides must be fair. It will do no good to see red.

"With immigration restricted, it will be necessary for business to seek another source of labor supply. This exists in the colored population. When they settle here and become workers in the community they have a right to a place to live amid conditions that insure health and sanitation.

"I know from experience that the negroes are not anxious to invade white residence districts any more than white people are willing that they should come."

The face of Julius Rosenwald softened.

"The negro is the equal of the white man in brains," said Mr. Rosenwald. "I have talked with men who said they started with a theory that the negro is inferior, but when the facts were arrived at, there was no other conclusion to be derived from those facts than that the colored man is the equal in intelligence of the white man.

"I attended the graduation ceremonies of this year's class at Hampton institute in May, the fifty-first anniversary of this negro institution. I heard Columbus K. Simango tell 'The South African's Story.' Here he was, straight from the jungles of Africa, a full blooded negro who came direct from Melsetter, South Rhodesia, to Hampton institute. His speech, his markings in classes, his general behavior showed intelligence and competency. He is a specimen of what can be accomplished by education.

"He didn't know he wanted an education till he met a missionary who told him about Hampton. He walked 200 miles to a port, and was started for America three times and then turned back by authorities. He arrived in America a grown young man, unable to read or write. And now he is able to pass any college examinations in America.

"Another speaker was a Fisk university man, Isaac Fisher. He has taken thirty-two prizes offered by newspapers and magazines in competitions open to all without regard to color. While living in Arkansas, he wrote to the St. Louis *Globe-Democrat* the twelve best reasons why Missouri is the best state to live in, and was awarded the prize. *Everybody's Magazine* had a contest with 3,000 competitors, and the award of $1,000 was made to Isaac Fisher, a type of the pure negro, a little thin fellow who is all intelligence."

Mr. Rosenwald quoted Walter Hines Page, a southerner, ambassador to Great Britain during the late war, "The most expensive thing we can do is not to educate the negro."

He quoted Booker Washington, from memory, as saying that in some southern states it was found that $16 per capita was spent on the education of white children in the public schools and $1.29 yearly on the colored children, and Washington's comment that such a disparity presumed too much on the intelligence of the eager blacks.

There are now more than 300 Rosenwald rural schools in operation in southern states, 300 more partially established and 400 others projected. They are maintained by three contributors, Mr. Rosenwald, state treasuries and miscellaneous donors.

[XVI]

FOR FEDERAL ACTION

THE race question is national and federal. No city or state can solve it alone. There must be coöperation between states. And there must be federal handling of it.

This is the view of Major Joel E. Spingarn, recently returned from service under fire in France and later service in the occupied zone in Germany with the 311th Infantry. Major Spingarn was for six years chairman of the National Association for the Advancement of Colored People.

"What is now happening in Chicago has happened in other large cities, north and south, east and west," said Major Spingarn. "With the initial or igniting occurrences out of consideration we have much the same developments in every case where there are race riots. Everything considered, the character of the Chicago population and the size of it, the total number of casualties is surprisingly low.

"The fact must now be emphasized that the race problem is not local, but is a national question. It should have federal attention, and there should be federal aid. We must fight as a national danger the race

[79]

hatred that exists in the south. That particular form of race hatred, which was one fundamental cause of the civil war, should not be permitted to spread to other sections.

"The southern neglect of the negro is a national problem. All the conditions of life that tend to degrade the negro in the south immediately come into evidence the moment there is a shift of negro population from south to north. Every circumstance of bad housing, bad sanitation, school neglect and economic inequality that exists in the southern states must be regarded as a national problem, this more especially in view of the shifts of population that are so easy now and which are sometimes an absolute necessity for the conduct of industry.

"There must be enlightenment of the intelligent whites of America on all phases of this problem. The intelligent white man who is not informed on the neglect and wrong training of the negro in the south is as dangerous to future peace and law and order as is the so-called bad negro. I have fought for my country two years as a major of infantry and I wish to give it as my mature judgment that no barbarities committed by the Prussians in Belgium will compare with the brutalities and atrocities committed on negroes in the south. In effect, you may say that the negroes who come north have issued from a system of life and industry far worse than anything ever seen under Prussianism in its worse manifestations.

"Every colored soldier that I have talked with in France, Germany or America has a grievance. If there should be a development of bolshevism in this country, it is plainly evident where these soldiers, at least those with whom I have talked, would take their stand.

"One of the most significant features in the Chicago situation is the stockyards labor union, and the apparent good will between the two races among the thousands of white and colored men in that organization. I am told that about 60 per cent of the stockyard workers are Poles, and that their leader, John Kirkulski, as well as the secretary and the 500 shop stewards of the organization, are taking a decisive stand against race prejudice, violence and anything else than peace and equality before the law.

"If this is true and it should be found that among the 70,000 men employed at the packing houses there has been no violence between white and colored union men, it may be that this is a high point in history. It is gratifying to hear that the employers at the stockyards recognized months ago that rivalries and bitterness between union white men and nonunion colored men would make a bad situation, and therefore they consented to the colored employment agencies recommending to all negroes applying for jobs that they should join the union. It is evident that without these stabilizing influences Chicago might have had a slaughter running into hundreds.

"A commission, consisting of men and women from

both races, should be appointed to investigate and make recommendations. Such a commission, if it has the right people on it, takes the thought of people away from violence. That was our experience in the Atlanta riots."

Printed in the United States
85106LV00002B/11/A

9 780151 171507